IN MY BLOOD

Words and Music by SHAWN MENDES,
GEOFF WARBURTON, TEDDY GEIGER
and SCOTT HARRIS

Slow, steady beat

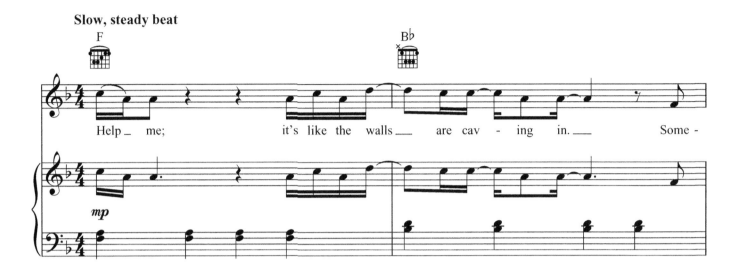

PIANO / VOCAL / GUITAR

SHAWN MENDES

ISBN: 978-1-5400-3131-0

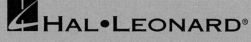

Visit Hal Leonard Online at
www.halleonard.com

Contact Us:
Hal Leonard
7777 West Bluemound Road
Milwaukee, WI 53213
Email: info@halleonard.com

In Europe contact:
Hal Leonard Europe Limited
42 Wigmore Street
Marylebone, London, W1U 2RN
Email: info@halleonardeurope.com

In Australia contact:
Hal Leonard Australia Pty. Ltd.
4 Lentara Court
Cheltenham, Victoria, 3192 Australia
Email: info@halleonard.com.au

NERVOUS

Words and Music by SHAWN MENDES,
SCOTT HARRIS and JULIA MICHAELS

With a groove

LOST IN JAPAN

Words and Music by SHAWN MENDES,
TEDDY GEIGER, NATE MERCEREAU
and SCOTT HARRIS

WHERE WERE YOU IN THE MORNING?

Words and Music by SHAWN MENDES,
SCOTT HARRIS, GEOFFREY WARBURTON
and TEDDY GEIGER

LIKE TO BE YOU

Words and Music by SHAWN MENDES,
SCOTT HARRIS and JULIA MICHAELS

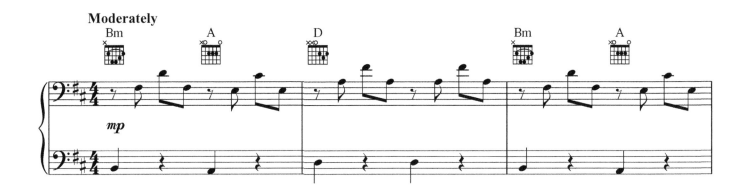

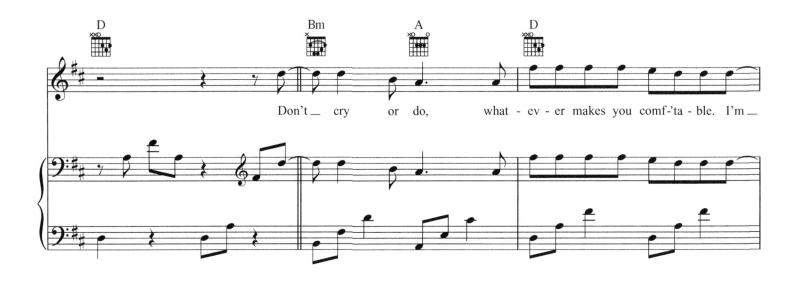

Don't __ cry or do, what-ev-er makes you comf-'ta-ble. I'm __

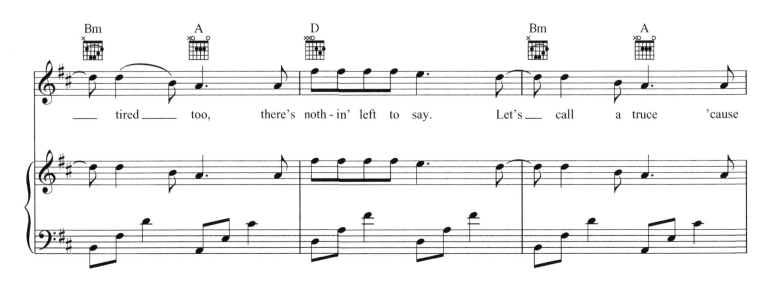

__ tired __ too, there's noth-in' left to say. Let's __ call a truce 'cause

PARTICULAR TASTE

Words and Music by SHAWN MENDES,
RYAN TEDDER and ZACH SKELTON

Acoustic groove

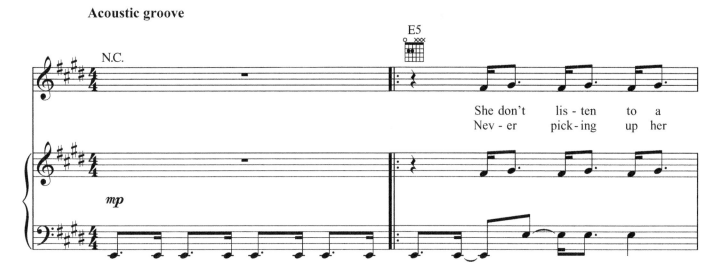

She don't lis-ten to a
Nev-er pick-ing up her

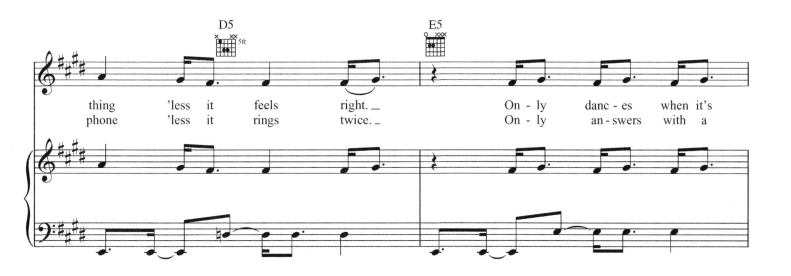

thing 'less it feels right. __ On-ly danc-es when it's
phone 'less it rings twice. __ On-ly an-swers with a

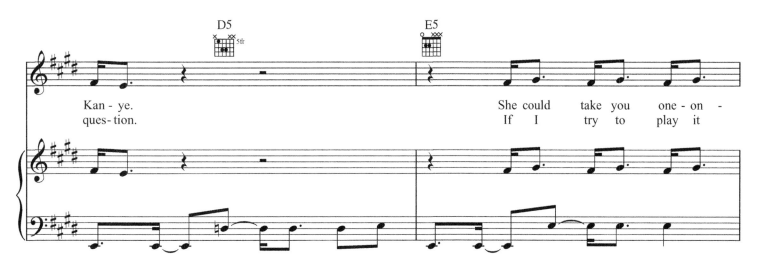

Kan-ye. She could take you one-on-
ques-tion. If I try to play it

FALLIN' ALL IN YOU

Words and Music by SHAWN MENDES,
JOHNNY McDAID, TEDDY GEIGER,
ED SHEERAN, FRED GIBSON
and SCOTT HARRIS

WHY

Words and Music by SHAWN MENDES,
TEDDY GEIGER and SCOTT HARRIS

BECAUSE I HAD YOU

Words and Music by SHAWN MENDES, TEDDY GEIGER,
SCOTT HARRIS, RYAN TEDDER
and ZACH SKELTON

YOUTH

Words and Music by SHAWN MENDES,
TEDDY GEIGER, GEOFF WARBURTON,
KHALID ROBINSON, SCOTT HARRIS
and NOLAN LAMBROZA

MUTUAL

Words and Music by SHAWN MENDES, TEDDY GEIGER,
SCOTT HARRIS, IAN KIRKPATRICK
and GEOFFREY WARBURTON

Acoustic Pop

I want you close to me, I want you close, I want you

clos - er. But when you're here with me,

it's hard to tell just what you're af - ter. You say __

PERFECTLY WRONG

Words and Music by SHAWN MENDES,
TEDDY GEIGER, SCOTT HARRIS
and GEOFFREY WARBURTON

D.S. al Coda

WHEN YOU'RE READY

Words and Music by SHAWN MENDES, TEDDY GEIGER,
SCOTT HARRIS, AMY ALLEN
and GEOFF WARBURTON

QUEEN

Words and Music by SHAWN MENDES,
TEDDY GEIGER, SCOTT HARRIS
and GEOFFREY WARBURTON

More Songbooks from Your Favorite Artists

ADELE – 25

22 songs: All I Ask • Hello – I Miss You • Million Years Ago • River Lea • Send My Love (To Your New Lover) • Water Under the Bridge • When We Were Young • and more.

00155393 Piano/Vocal/Guitar $19.99

SARA BAREILLES – AMIDST THE CHAOS

12 songs: Armor • Fire • No Such Thing • Poetry by Dead Men • A Safe Place to Land (feat. John Legend) • Saint Honesty • and more.

00294277 Piano/Vocal/Guitar $19.99

LEWIS CAPALDI – DIVINELY UNINSPIRED TO A HELLISH EXTENT

Bruises • Don't Get Me Wrong • Fade • Forever • Grace • Headspace • Hold Me While You Wait • Hollywood • Lost on You • Maybe • One • Someone You Loved.

00299905 Piano/Vocal/Guitar $19.99

COLDPLAY – EVERYDAY LIFE

16 tracks featuring the title track plus: Arabesque • Broken • Champion of the World • Church • Cry Cry Cry • Daddy • Eko • Guns • Sunrise • When I Need a Friend • and more.

00327962 Piano/Vocal/Guitar $19.99

BILLIE EILISH – WHEN WE ALL FALL ASLEEP, WHERE DO WE GO?

13 songs: All the Good Girls Go to Hell • Bad Guy • Bury a Friend • 8 • Goodbye • I Love You • ilomilo • Listen Before I Go • My Strange Addiction • When the Party's Over • Wish You Were Gay • Xanny • You Should See Me in a Crown.

00295684 Piano/Vocal/Guitar $19.99

ARIANA GRANDE – THANK U, NEXT

11 songs: Bad Idea • Bloodline • Break up with Your Girlfriend, I'm Bored • Fake Smile • Ghostin • Imagine • In My Head • Make Up • NASA • Needy • 7 Rings.

00292769 Piano/Vocal/Guitar $19.99

LIZZO – CUZ I LOVE YOU

12 songs: Better in Color • Crybaby • Cuz I Love You • Exactly How I Feel • Heaven Help Me • Jerome • Juice • Like a Girl • Lingerie • Soulmate • Tempo • Truth Hurts.

00304758 Piano/Vocal/Guitar $19.99

THE LUMINEERS – III

13 songs: April • Democracy • Donna • Gloria • It Wasn't Easy to Be Happy for You • Jimmy Sparks • Leader of the Landslide • Left for Denver • Life in the City • My Cell • Old Lady • Salt and the Sea • Soundtrack Song.

00322983 Piano/Vocal/Guitar $19.99

SHAWN MENDES

14 songs: Because I Had You • Fallin' All in You • In My Blood • Like to Be You • Lost in Japan • Mutual • Nervous • Particular Taste • Perfectly Wrong • Queen • When You're Ready, I'm Waiting • Where Were You in the Morning? • Why • Youth.

00279536 Piano/Vocal/Guitar $17.99

HARRY STYLES – FINE LINE

12 songs: Adore You • Canyon Moon • Cherry • Falling • Fine Line • Golden • Lights Up • She • Sunflower, Vol. 6 • To Be So Lonely • Treat People with Kindness • Watermelon Sugar.

00338558 Piano/Vocal/Guitar $19.99

TAYLOR SWIFT – FOLKLORE

17 songs: Betty • Cardigan • Exile (feat. Bon Iver) • Illicit Affairs • The Lakes • The Last Great American Dynasty • Mad Woman • The 1 • Peace • and more.

00356804 Piano/Vocal/Guitar $19.99

HAL•LEONARD®

For a complete listing of the products available, visit us online at **www.halleonard.com**

Contents, prices, and availability subject to change without notice.

0920
015

THE NEW DECADE SERIES

Books with Online Audio • Arranged for Piano, Voice, and Guitar

The New Decade Series features collections of iconic songs from each decade with great backing tracks so you can play them and sound like a pro. You access the tracks online for streaming or download. **See complete song listings online at www.halleonard.com**

SONGS OF THE 1920s
Ain't Misbehavin' • Baby Face • California, Here I Come • Fascinating Rhythm • I Wanna Be Loved by You • It Had to Be You • Mack the Knife • Ol' Man River • Puttin' on the Ritz • Rhapsody in Blue • Someone to Watch over Me • Tea for Two • Who's Sorry Now • and more.
00137576 P/V/G.....................................$24.99

SONGS OF THE 1930s
As Time Goes By • Blue Moon • Cheek to Cheek • Embraceable You • A Fine Romance • Georgia on My Mind • I Only Have Eyes for You • The Lady Is a Tramp • On the Sunny Side of the Street • Over the Rainbow • Pennies from Heaven • Stormy Weather (Keeps Rainin' All the Time) • The Way You Look Tonight • and more.
00137579 P/V/G.....................................$24.99

SONGS OF THE 1940s
At Last • Boogie Woogie Bugle Boy • Don't Get Around Much Anymore • God Bless' the Child • How High the Moon • It Could Happen to You • La Vie En Rose (Take Me to Your Heart Again) • Route 66 • Sentimental Journey • The Trolley Song • You'd Be So Nice to Come Home To • Zip-A-Dee-Doo-Dah • and more.
00137582 P/V/G.....................................$24.99

SONGS OF THE 1950s
Ain't That a Shame • Be-Bop-A-Lula • Chantilly Lace • Earth Angel • Fever • Great Balls of Fire • Love Me Tender • Mona Lisa • Peggy Sue • Que Sera, Sera (Whatever Will Be, Will Be) • Rock Around the Clock • Sixteen Tons • A Teenager in Love • That'll Be the Day • Unchained Melody • Volare • You Send Me • Your Cheatin' Heart • and more.
00137595 P/V/G.....................................$24.99

SONGS OF THE 1960s
All You Need Is Love • Beyond the Sea • Born to Be Wild • California Girls • Dancing in the Street • Happy Together • King of the Road • Leaving on a Jet Plane • Louie, Louie • My Generation • Oh, Pretty Woman • Sunshine of Your Love • Under the Boardwalk • You Really Got Me • and more.
00137596 P/V/G $24.99

SONGS OF THE 1970s
ABC • Bridge over Troubled Water • Cat's in the Cradle • Dancing Queen • Free Bird • Goodbye Yellow Brick Road • Hotel California • I Will Survive • Joy to the World • Killing Me Softly with His Song • Layla • Let It Be • Piano Man • The Rainbow Connection • Stairway to Heaven • The Way We Were • Your Song • and more.
00137599 P/V/G $27.99

SONGS OF THE 1980s
Addicted to Love • Beat It • Careless Whisper • Come on Eileen • Don't Stop Believin' • Every Rose Has Its Thorn • Footloose • I Just Called to Say I Love You • Jessie's Girl • Livin' on a Prayer • Saving All My Love for You • Take on Me • Up Where We Belong • The Wind Beneath My Wings • and more.
00137600 P/V/G...................................$27.99

SONGS OF THE 1990s
Angel • Black Velvet • Can You Feel the Love Tonight • (Everything I Do) I Do It for You • Friends in Low Places • Hero • I Will Always Love You • More Than Words • My Heart Will Go On (Love Theme from 'Titanic') • Smells like Teen Spirit • Under the Bridge • Vision of Love • Wonderwall • and more.
00137601 P/V/G...................................$27.99

SONGS OF THE 2000s
Bad Day • Beautiful • Before He Cheats • Chasing Cars • Chasing Pavements • Drops of Jupiter (Tell Me) • Fireflies • Hey There Delilah • How to Save a Life • I Gotta Feeling • I'm Yours • Just Dance • Love Story • 100 Years • Rehab • Unwritten • You Raise Me Up • and more.
00137608 P/V/G...................................$27.99

SONGS OF THE 2010s
All About That Bass • All of Me • Brave • Empire State of Mind • Get Lucky • Happy • Hey, Soul Sister • I Knew You Were Trouble • Just the Way You Are • Need You Now • Pompeii • Radioactive • Rolling in the Deep • Shake It Off • Shut up and Dance • Stay with Me • Take Me to Church • Thinking Out Loud • Uptown Funk • and many more.
00151836 P/V/G $27.99

halleonard.com
Prices, content, and availability subject to change without notice.